The Monthly Partner

Discovering the hidden relationships
that advance
your organization's future

By John R. Frank, CFRE
with Mark Cutshall

Steward Publishing
Woodinville, Washington

The Monthly Partner:
Discovering the hidden relationships
that advance your organization's future

First Edition

Steward Publishing
14642 N.E. 174th St.
Woodinville, Wash. 98072
U.S.A.
www.JohnRFrank.com

ISBN 0-9754399-1-X

Cover design by Paul Graves, DOXA Total Design Strategy, Inc., www.doxa.biz

Printed in the United States of America

10 9 8 7 6 5 4 3 2 1

Acknowledgements

After finishing my first book, *The Ministry of Development*, I realized how much work goes into the production of each new work. I am thankful to the team effort to produce a book, no matter how small or large an effort.

First, I want to thank my family, Susan, Kyle and Sarah. My family is why I do what I do. They are my first line of support.

Then, to my new close friend Mark Cutshall, thank you. I have known Mark a number of years, but this is our first collaboration. What a gifted man. I could not have finished this without him.

To my team of John, Scott, Diane, Shannon, Leon, Monroe, Stan and Bud I say thanks for your support, wisdom and passion. My life is enriched working with you.

And to my God and Savior, I am thankful for life every day.

John R. Frank

Contents

Introduction

The CEO of a leading relief and development organization summed up his day before his first cup of coffee had a chance to cool. Opening the door of his office, he looked at his watch, smiled at his assistant and said, "It's 8 a.m. By the time this month is over we'll need to raise $100,000 – and keep bringing in $100,000 each month thereafter throughout the rest of the year to stay alive."

What about you? The questions I ask every prospective client are the same ones I'll ask you:

How much will your organization need to raise this year?
How are you going to raise the needed gifts?
What's your plan?

Did you know that a critical element of any successful development/fundraising plan is an overlooked, underutilized strategy called the Monthly Partner Program that can:

- increase your total annual income
- create a predictable monthly revenue
- build a better, lasting relationship with your most faithful donors
- increase their longevity, as donors, by 50 percent, and
- lower your fundraising costs.

The Monthly Partner Program is a proven, systematic fundraising approach. It offers your regular, frequent donors a convenient way to give, honors their consistent generosity and solidifies a long-term relationship with your organization.

To understand and appreciate the Monthly Partner Program, you need to see its unique, invaluable place in the big picture of development:

1

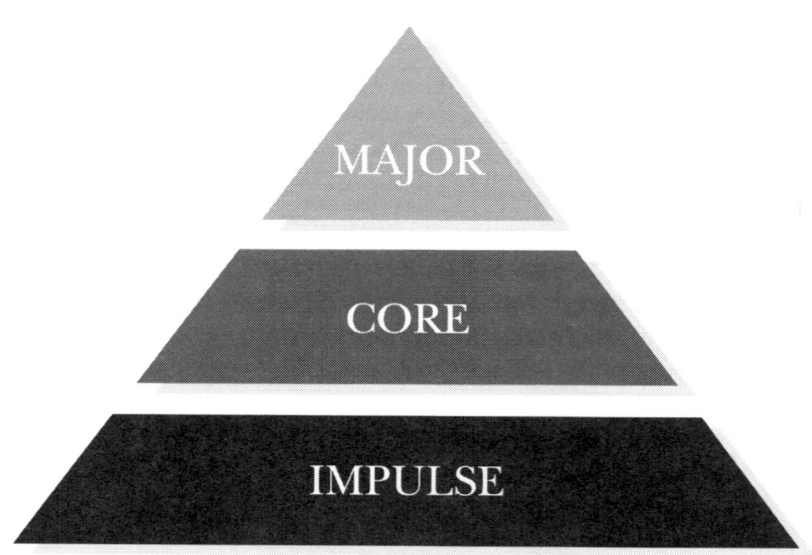

This is the Donor Pyramid, and it's foundational to a sound development strategy for all nonprofit organizations. The Donor Pyramid represents the people who give to your organization – and it represents those who have the financial resources to take your organization to the next level.

The top section signifies your major donors. No doubt you know their names. They're the generous individuals and families who typically give large amounts once or twice a year. Normally, the collective gifts of an organization's major donors make up 30-50 percent of your total annual gift income. Your major donors are essential to your overall development effort, but this group is only one important piece of the puzzle.

You'll see that the bottom section represents your impulse donors. Their single contribution can be a fraction of a major donor gift. Yet you need them because, while the amounts may be modest, impulse donors typically outnumber all other types of donors.

This brings us to the middle tier of the Donor Pyramid – your core donors. They are your organization's most faithful, consistent givers whose donations have been coming in regularly for months and years.

Every single donor is important to your organization. Each one wants to be appreciated. Each one deserves to be thanked. Each one needs to be valued. Yet I believe one group of donors probably gets the least amount of attention. Their underutilized participation in your organization might be hindering new growth and minimizing your ministry's impact.

These often overlooked donors are your monthly partners. Their faithfulness – and their ability to transform your organization – is why I wrote this book. Your monthly partners are the "forgotten faithful." In the next few pages, you're going to discover what their undeterred loyalty can mean to your ministry.

You are going to see how the character and commitment of these people already giving to your ministry, along with many more who are ready to give, illustrate timeless biblical principles. Their remarkable stories exemplify a proven fundraising strategy that has worked successfully for many ministry organizations – and can work for your group.

It's called the Monthly Partner Program. It's absolutely essential to the financial health and well-being of your organization. Why? Because to meet ongoing program needs and to make commitments, payroll and other expenses, you need predictable income. Major donors provide significant resources, and the sheer numbers of your impulse donors can't be ignored. Yet inside the Donor Pyramid the greatest potential source for needed, regular income rests with your core donors.

And at the center of your core donors are your all-important monthly partners.

I want to be very clear: If you fail to create a Monthly Partner Program – more specifically, if you currently do not have such a program in place:

- You are leaving a significant amount of donations on the table.
- You are ignoring donors who want to give to you consistently.
- You are missing out on a fundraising opportunity that could amount to 5 to 25 percent of your total gift income.

But more importantly, without a Monthly Partner Program in place, you are missing out on building hundreds, perhaps thousands of cherished relationships. Ignoring a Monthly Partner Program means ignoring the people who can and will stand with your organization through good times and bad, people who can and will give to you and pray for you now and for years to come.

A Monthly Partner Program is all about creating consistent revenue and building long-term donor relationships – through a growing family of loyal supporters who share your mission and vision and who will give generously over months and years to make it happen.

The Monthly Partner Program really is one expression of a total approach I call "the ministry of development." For nonprofit organizations, development encompasses much more than fundraising. At its core, development is simply people helping people.

More specifically, the ministry of development means creating opportunities to involve God's people in God's work. This process links people who believe in God and His Kingdom work on earth with the work itself. Within the context of the ministry of development, a Monthly Partner Program allows you to link loyal donors with your organization's Kingdom work.

This book gives you everything to create and sustain a successful Monthly Partner Program. This is not some instant fundraising technique – "just add water and stir." It requires work. And if you follow this step-by-step plan, you can take your organization to the next level by drawing closer to your donors in ways you never imagined.

To understand and execute the three essential phases of the Monthly Partner Program, here is a chapter-by-chapter overview of the content we will cover:

SETTING THE STAGE
The proper focus for generating lasting results

Chapter One
Relationships: The Heart and Soul of a Monthly Partner Program
Chapter Two
Identifying the Donor Prospect

BUILDING THE PROGRAM
A proven, step-by-step approach

Chapter Three
The Six Essential Elements
Chapter Four
The Invitation to Join
Chapter Five
The Management System

PUTTING IT INTO ACTION
The invaluable tools you need to begin

At the end of each chapter you will find an important list of "Action Items." These practical steps make up a comprehensive "Action Item Master Plan" found in Chapter Ten.

The moment has arrived
Where does a Monthly Partner Program begin? With *you*, especially if you are:

- an executive director of a nonprofit organization who is wearing multiple hats – including one that says "Development"
- a full-time development director of a small- to medium-size group
- a development officer responsible for donor relationships, cultivating new gift income from new sources
- a board member on the development committee looking for new strategies
- a volunteer involved in a start-up effort, or working to hire and build your first staff

Let's lay out this proven fundraising approach that can cause you to smile at the bottom line each month and, more importantly, help you celebrate something ultimately more valuable. What I want to share with you, now, is at the very heart of the Monthly Partner Program, and it can take your organization to the next level of donor support.

SETTING THE STAGE
The proper focus for generating lasting results

When it comes to creating a lasting relationship with your donors, the right perspective is everything. Chapters One and Two give you the "big picture" of the Monthly Partner Program so you can see what is really at stake between your organization and your loyal donors.

❦

Chapter One
Relationships:
The Heart and Soul of a Monthly Partner Program

Recently, I came across a statement that stopped me cold:

If you doubt the power of advertising, then consider this fact: There are 25 mountains in the Colorado Rockies higher than Pikes Peak. Can you name one of them?

Your fundraising challenge is a lot like the Rockies and the surrounding terrain. For every major "Pike's Peak" (or "big name") donor, there are dozens, perhaps hundreds of other donors who remain anonymous. These are your core donors. While they may lack prominence, their consistent, generous loyalty is vital to achieving your funding goals.

Look, again, at the "range" of everyone who gives to your organization and you will see why you need all three types of donors – major, impulse and core. The temptation, for some leaders, is to "go to the top" and focus enormous attention and effort on the major donors. You can become preoccupied with Pike's Peak, the "name" donor who, for whatever reason, captures an excessive amount of your time – and fail to see the rest of the development landscape.

There's a second temptation. Conversely, you can focus on the hinterlands, the multitude of impulse donors "in the valley," and mistakenly miss the opportunity to go after larger gifts. Either way, you can miss out on the broad expanse right before your eyes. In the ministry of development, this means having a complete appreciation for *all* of your donors–major, impulse and core.

Keep that "big picture" in mind as we focus on the Monthly Partner Program. In this chapter I want you to consider your core donors, more specifically your monthly partners, whose names you may not even know, yet whose individual, regular contributions your organization simply can't live without.

In this chapter you are going to learn:

- Why the time is right for a Monthly Partner Program
- What makes the MPP distinct from a traditional donor appeal

Hungering for something more

The overcrowded, rush-rush American culture in which your donors live is ripe for the Monthly Partner Program. Here is why:

Years ago, if you wanted to take up a cause, raise money and fulfill a dream, you went out and basically did it. Take my mother. Back in the 1960s, she developed a growing passion for feeding seniors in our hometown of Cross Plains, Wisconsin. At the local school cafeteria, she helped create a hot lunch program for needy elderly residents. She got the word out and scores of people showed up. It was so successful that eventually the program went statewide.

My dad had his own dream. Our little community of 1,600 had no community pool. He helped organize a ballot measure and galvanized the support of enough voters who said "yes" to build a pool with their modest tax dollars. I still remember walking off the dimensions of the pool with Dad and being one of the first kids to jump in on that glorious opening day.

Our world, the world in which your donors live, work and play, has changed. Today, populations are more diverse. Neighborhoods aren't as simple as they used to be. The "good ol' days" of pausing to read the newspaper on the front porch have been eclipsed by a daily bombardment of interruptions and noise. For example, consider what your donors woke up to this morning. Long before they thought about your organization, they were hit with wake-up alarms, chirping cell phones, cable news commentators and loud school bells. And that's just before 9:00 a.m.!

All of this collective static is exactly what your donors *don't* want – one more impersonal appeal, one more come-on, one more sales pitch from a telemarketer bouncing his wares off your eardrum just as you're sitting down to dinner.

Your donors are hungry for something different. They are human beings with real feelings and desires. Like you and me they want to be appreciated and valued. When it comes to your organization, they don't want to feel like one more number on a mailing list.

Instead, what they really want is a relationship.

Your donors want to belong to a cause that is consistent with their values, passion and faith. They want to give to organizations they believe are doing work that is worthy and good. This is why your donors are already giving to your organization! In your group they see something that rings true with their own heartfelt concerns, their stories, their lives.

The time is right for creating a Monthly Partner Program because this is an approach that connects your donors' desire for lasting, meaningful relationships with an organization like yours that affirms their values and concerns.

A Monthly Partner Program is a strategic, step-by-step plan that identifies and secures the financial support of faithful core donors who will give to your organization consistently over time and whose collective contributions can total as much as 10-25 percent of your annual donor income.

The Monthly Partner Program works because it fulfills the four primary needs of every core donor, namely the need to:

- be thanked and appreciated for their past support
- feel special by being invited to belong to an "insiders' group"
- know they are making a life-changing difference and
- give in a convenient, simple means that best fits their home finance pattern and preferences.

The heart of the Monthly Partner Program is the clear, consistent message you send to every partner each month:

- You are incredibly important to our ministry.
- You are so important, in fact, that your loyal commitment deserves a special place in our organization.
- Your faithfulness, your relationship with us, means everything to our organization – and the people whose lives you are helping to change.

The Monthly Partner Program is not a monthly fund appeal. Rather, it is a monthly affirmation to donors who already are behind you, a reminder that your organization is living out their values and ideals. Your monthly communication, along with a return envelope, prearranged agreement for electronic funds transfer (EFT) or online giving offers a consistent, convenient means for donors to continue making their contributions. (You will learn exactly how this system works later on.)

For now, here are the two most important things to remember about this all-important first phase of "Setting the Stage":

- The time is right for the Monthly Partner Program because more than ever, in an increasingly noisy world, people desire a relationship with organizations that honor, value and appreciate them.
- The Monthly Partner Program works for donors because it offers them a convenient means to enjoy a meaningful relationship with your organization by being part of an insiders' group.

Whether they number in the tens, the hundreds or the thousands, your core donors have shown they not only want to give to your organization, they want to keep giving. And they may well increase their regular monthly giving if you know where they're coming from. It's all there in the research. . . .

Action Items:
To make this chapter count toward your Monthly Partner Program:
1. Meet with your key leadership to present the Monthly Partner Program.
2. Obtain buy-in and consensus for the program from your leadership.
3. Make the decision to start!

Chapter Two

The Six Essential Elements

Has this ever happened to you: It's one o' clock in the morning, and you've just finished watching a mystery thriller. You're about ready to click off the television, when you make a calculated mistake to channel surf. Within a few seconds you're glued to the set – and hooked by an infomercial. Not only are you watching, you're (gasp!) trying to write down the toll-free number!

You can laugh at these late-night infomercials all you want – except the successful ones. There is a secret about them you need to know: Each one follows a winning formula, a proven approach. The same principle is true when creating an effective Monthly Partner Program.

In this chapter you are going to learn:

- the six essential elements of a successful Monthly Partner Program, and
- why each one helps you set the stage for your program.

While I didn't invent the Monthly Partner Program, I know this approach inside and out. The same six foundational elements that have comprised each program I've ever led can help you achieve the most attentive attitude and productive focus for your own upcoming program. Let's take a close look at each element. . . .

#1 – Think "win-win"

Your Monthly Partner Program is designed to create a "win-win" for your organization *and* the donor. A mutually-rewarding outcome is the goal and essence of your program. Aim to create the best possible outcome for your donor and you will put your organization in position to receive the best possible result.

Consistent, loyal givers in your program "win" by:

- playing a part to keep the organization financially stable
- focusing their giving to areas of ministry they care about
- realizing their regular, small gifts make a big impact over time
- knowing their faithful participation encourages your team
- enjoying the convenience of monthly reminders, electronic funds transfer or online giving and
- being part of a group of insiders who feel close to the organization

Simultaneously, your organization "wins" through:
- consistent cash flow bringing stability
- loyal donors who plan to stand with you for the long haul and
- growing trust, goodwill and allegiance within your current donors who can't help but tell others.

#2 – Know your target segment

Which people are drawn to a Monthly Partner Program? Much of the answer has to do with certain generational distinctives of your prospective donors (more about this later). It is essential to get a profile of three distinctive types of donors and know their respective preferences toward monthly giving. You can increase your program's potential success by paying attention to demographics (age and life stage) and psychographics (behavior patterns) of each target segment.

Donors who like to save time will be drawn to the Monthly Partner Program because it's quick and convenient.

Donors who currently give on a regular basis are a perfect match for the Monthly Partner Program because it affirms their demonstrated loyalty.

Donors who love your organization, yet whose giving is inconsistent, can become Monthly Partner Program members through monthly reminders that make their "love" a monthly habit.

Donors who give three or four times a year will, through the Monthly Partner Program, be able to deepen their commitment to your organization as monthly givers.

Donors who give $100 or more annually will consider the Monthly Partner Program a way to continue their commitment on a more regular basis and total more on an annual basis.

Regardless of their generation, builder, boomer and buster donors will consider (and join) the Monthly Partner Program when they can give in the manner they're most comfortable with, whether by check, online or electronic funds transfer.

#3 – Value designated giving

Monthly partners who commit to give on a monthly basis care very deeply about an organization. Because of this, they may want to choose where their giving goes. I consulted with one rescue mission that already had a giving program focused on feeding and sheltering the homeless. When we launched their new Monthly Partner Program, the donors wrote that they wanted to make sure their gifts were still going toward feeding and sheltering the needy and not to other general needs and program costs of the organization. We assured these donors we would honor their "designated wishes."

Not all donors want such directed giving. In fact, many organizations and churches do not allow designated giving because it can restrict the management of finances. Still, designated giving is a trend that can't be reversed. In your own Monthly Partner Program, you can create one or two designated areas, along with your general needs. This "happy medium" can speak to both the "directed" and "overall" inclinations of your donors, without disregarding either preference.

#4 – Create a compelling name

Like the irresistible title of a good book, the name of your Monthly Partner Program is all-important. And unlike a book that goes out of print, the name of a successful program is bound to have some extended shelf life.

What makes a good name? First, it should reflect the quality relationship your organization wants to build with your donors. The name should ring true to the cause and concerns of your organization and strike a chord with the donor.

Second, a Monthly Partner Program name should carry some emotional weight and tie in to the "front lines" of your organization – the place where your people touch the point of need.

Here are a few examples from the "Hall of Names" of organizations I have been privileged to serve:

A rescue mission located near the town's marine port used a lighthouse as its logo to suggest safety and direction to the homeless. The program was named the "Safe Harbor Club."

Jesus' parable of the shepherd who looked for (and found!) the one lost sheep inspired an urban rescue mission to name its monthly partner program the "99 & One Club."

Another rescue mission wanted to draw its monthly partners closer to the emotional heart of its work with the homeless by honoring each member-donor as a "Friend of the Friendless."

A youth ministry turned the local teenage gang presence into a positive by naming its monthly partner program the "Takin' It to the Streets Gang."

#5 – Take the initiative

The Monthly Partner Program is distinct from direct-mail campaigns. It is *not* a monthly appeal. You don't have to "sell" your donors on your organization. Remember, because of their past giving, whether regular or sporadic, your donors are already "in your camp." What they need is a regular reminder and thank-you that their faithful monthly giving is helping to change lives.

As an organization, you can't afford to wait around and expect your donors "somewhere out there" to give. However, by taking the initiative with a timely, personal reminder you can meet the needs of your donor:

- Donors with active lifestyles (the "boomers" and "busters" you will learn more about later) are often distracted by the stuff of life. A gentle, respectful reminder of the commitment they have already made is very accepted. In fact, many donors view your regular follow-up as a reaffirmation of how your organization is a wise steward of their gifts.

- Elderly donors, those in the "builder" generation, may initially be put off by a monthly reminder. They may see it as bill collecting. This "senior" generation is faithful in giving and does not need reminding. Even so, your personable monthly reminders can lead them to look forward to new, inspiring, life-changing stories. Your reminders can be the well-timed reaffirmation of their continuous support.

#6 – Create the inner circle

In a recent research project, donors were asked what would draw them closer to an organization which they currently support. The number one response was, "If I contact the leadership and receive a reply."

People want to be involved in the ministries they support. They long for caring, satisfying relationships. They want to know their giving matters and that there are equally-concerned folks on the other end (a president, CEO, manager, team leader and staff) who value them as people, not merely as a signature on a check.

The Monthly Partner Program does away with this ill-fated perception for good! Not only do people want to be valued, your donors will feel even more special and appreciated by being part of a gathering of like-minded people with shared values. By belonging to the "inner circle" they can accomplish something remarkable together, something they could not achieve on their own.

Therefore, an essential ingredient of your Monthly Partner Program is the creation of an "inner circle" of supporters. One of the most powerful appeals is to belong to a select group. One of the most powerful things you can say to a donor is, "I want to invite you to be a part of a select group of individuals who share your passion and concern for . . ."

Consider "the big six" for yourself

These six essentials are the foundational walls upon which to build your Monthly Partner Program. They're so important, I want you to take a few minutes to discuss them with your immediate team. With each of these six essential ingredients ask, "How does this point ring true, individually or as an organization?"

Watch your best ideas begin to grow as you address the action items below. Discuss them freely and write them down. They'll be tremendously helpful to you as you move along and as you set the stage and get ready to build your Monthly Partner Program.

Action Items:

To make this chapter count toward your Monthly Partner Program:
1. Identify and prioritize the donor benefits of your Monthly Partner Program. (You will articulate these later in your brochure, see Chapter Four.)
2. Become familiar with your target segment.

3. List possible projects your Monthly Partner Program can fund.
4. Come up with a program name that reflects the loyalty of your donors and the front-line impact on those your organization serves.
5. Create a mailing schedule with key production deadlines for sending out your monthly reminder. (More about this in Chapter Five).
6. Brainstorm some creative ways you can appeal to the "inner circle" (from among your core donors) and draw them closer to the life-changing impact of your organization.

BUILDING THE PROGRAM

A proven, step-by-step approach

The effectiveness of the Monthly Partner Program rests on a carefully laid sequence. Chapters Three through Eight detail this straightforward plan, complete with how-tos, case study illustrations and tips to help you carry out each important step.

❦

Chapter Three

Identifying the Donor Prospect

Whenever I begin to talk about some of my clients' successes with the Monthly Partner Program, people want to know, "How does it work? How can *our* group do that? . . . Where do we start?"

The starting point is your donors.

The world of your donors is not only crowded, busy and forever running late to the next meeting – it's also shaped by some very significant generational perspectives.

"What's that term you just used, John? Generational *what?*" you ask.

Generational perspectives. Your Monthly Partner Program can be extremely effective, but only if you know the mindset and motivation of your donor. By knowing the generation to which your donor belongs, you can learn how to make each feel welcome, comfortable and fulfilled by giving to your organization. But I'm getting ahead of myself.

Because knowing your donor is foundational, this chapter will show you:

- three cultural trends driving the Monthly Partner Program
- three primary types of donors who can give to your organization
- how the Monthly Partner Program can involve them all.

Significant trend or passing fancy?
Do you know the difference between a fad and a trend? A fad is a passing fancy. A trend is a significant cultural shift. A fad is an "all the rage" rush to buy decorator matchsticks. A trend, on the other hand, is the emerging pattern of families who gather around the fire to share stories and songs. Fads burn out within a few weeks. Trends shape society over the course of years.

At least three significant cultural trends are at the root of the Monthly Partner Program. The *first* is the growing need and desire for people to feel included. Remember, we don't want to be known as a number. We want to be valued for our individual worth. We want to know our lives count.

But it goes deeper than that. Everyone wants to feel special. We want to feel that we belong, and that we are giving to something bigger than ourselves. We want to be on the "in" side of things. It is no coincidence that, several years ago, television shows with names like "Inside Edition" began to pop up. (In Chapter Eight you will learn how this "inside" approach is linked to your Monthly Partner Program.)

The *second* significant trend is the changing mindset in leadership and follower-ship. With so much scrutiny being paid to today's leaders – their ethics, personal lives, foibles and failures – donors want to know where their gifts are going. Donors are more curious, more involved and more inquiring than ever. ("How is my monthly gift making a difference?" is the perfect question that a successful Monthly Partner Program answers in Chapter Four.)

A *third* significant trend is our unending information overload. Donors can no longer remember all of the causes they support. Organizations that "get" this fact know how to make a home for their cause in the donor's mind. The moral of the story: If you make it easy for a donor to remember you when it comes time to write the monthly check, the donor will give like clockwork.

These three trends provide the backdrop to the differing generational perspectives mentioned earlier.

Three generational realities
A lot has been written about the distinctive views and attitudes of donors based on the generation into which they were born. So what does a

person's era or age mean for your organization? More than you can count.

Builders

The builder generation includes men and women born between 1920 and 1940. Known as "The War Generation," and revered by many as "The Greatest Generation," they literally built many of our nonprofit organizations, ministries and churches.

By and large, they believe in their leaders. Generally, they are trusting of authority figures. They tend to give unconditionally because they believe what their leaders tell them. Moreover, they believe the organizations they support will do the good and right things with their gifts.

Builders believe strongly in biblical stewardship. Sacrificial giving is an important part of their faith journey.

Boomers

The boomer generation was born after World War II, when affluence and consumerism spread throughout America. Boomers were raised by parents who wanted to give them a better world than they had. In effect, Mom and Dad wanted to give them everything. The boomers gladly obliged and have become accustomed to having everything they want – when they want it.

Thanks in part to divisive historical markers like Watergate and the Vietnam War, Boomers have learned not to trust political, religious or business leaders. The fallout, when it comes to fundraising, is that they want to direct, or designate, their giving. Boomers want accountable results. They are wealthier than any previous generation, and time is more valuable than money. Make it easy and time-efficient for boomers to give and they will tend to keep giving for a long time.

Busters

The buster generation, also referred to as "Generation X," was born after 1965 and is the first to believe that society (and their own lives) will not be as good as the previous generation. They believe the boomers have "used up everything." Their giving has a more hands-on approach. They tend to be skeptical, asking, "Will my giving will really make a difference?"

Like the boomers, busters are unsure of leadership and are not that concerned with an organization's "marketing strategies." Technologically astute, many busters do not use checkbooks, relying instead on on-line services to bank, buy and give to their charities of choice.

With these generational realities as a backdrop, how would you begin to describe your prospective Monthly Partner Program members?

The Monthly Partner Program has built-in characteristics that can address the priorities and values of each of these three sizeable generations:

- An effective program honors donors by acknowledging faithful stewardship. For this reason alone builders respond to a Monthly Partner Program.
- Because gifts made through the program are targeted and measured, boomer and buster generations tend to respond favorably.
- Boomers and busters value results: "Can the work of the organization be measured? . . . Will the organization share the results? . . . Can my giving be connected to results?" With a Monthly Partner Program the answer to each of these questions is an emphatic, "Yes!"

Why has the Monthly Partner Program worked for so many nonprofit groups? Because, first and foremost, it focuses on the donor – and meets the needs of the donor. And identifying the donor prospect is the first step.

Action Items:
To make this chapter count toward your Monthly Partner Program:
1. Find your donors who are currently giving monthly. These are the donors you will "honor in."
2. Do a search of your data base for donors who have give three, four or more times this past year.
3. Identify the builders, boomers and busters among your donor base.
4. Spot demographic, cultural and lifestyle trends in your community that may affect giving to your organization.

20

Chapter Four

An Invitation to Join

It's one of those moments you never forget. You're back in elementary school standing on the playground, and the team captain choosing sides looks your way and says, "I want you." Talk about a feeling of being affirmed and included.

It's not at all like coming home after a long day at work and being greeted by a stack of mail all addressed to "Occupant," "Resident," or "The family living at . . ."

Suddenly, one envelope catches your eye. You notice the return address, open the envelope and begin to read. The president of a homeless shelter you've supported for years is inviting you to join a select group in a new effort to offer homeless mothers in your community the safety, security and positive future they've never had.

The need is real. The message is honest and clear. The invitation to respond is irresistible, because a leader you respect has asked you to advance a cause you care deeply about. You feel appreciated on a whole new level, because someone says to you, "You're important. Our relationship with you and this organization means everything. As part of a select group of valued friends, you can make a life-changing difference."

The satisfaction of being chosen, the sense of belonging and the reward that comes from joining others in a life-transforming cause is why your donors will say "Yes" to your invitation to join your Monthly Partner Program.

- What's the best way to make that invitation?
- How can you maximize the participation of your current donors in this new campaign?
- What are the demonstrated approaches that can involve your faithful supporters in a way that strengthen their relationship with your organization so, together, you can further your group's dedicated cause?

The answers are lodged in three fundamentals. Let's examine each of them.

1. Qualify your audience

Your Monthly Partner Program starts with your list of current core donors who meet one of these criteria:

Frequency. Generally, core donors are those who give three to four or more times a year. They are not the major donors who give a large annual sum, nor are they the impulse donors who give a very modest amount in intermittent fashion.

Amount. The dollar total differs based on the size of your organization. As a practical rule of thumb, select the donors who have given $100 or more throughout the past 12-15 months. If a donor gives $35 three times a year, he or she would be a prospect for your Monthly Partner Program. FYI: Over the course of a year, a regular monthly gift of $35 would total $420, a 300% increase over the donor's previous annual giving.

Psychographics. You can increase your monthly partner prospect list by identifying donor patterns and organizational involvement. Such psychographic indicators can both validate an individual's place as a monthly partner prospect *and* identify new prospects who might be considered "borderline" based on frequency and amount. Here's how to bring this knowledge to light:

Assemble your development team around a table, making sure each person has a list of all your organization's current donors, including their giving records throughout the past 12 to 15 months. A certain number of monthly partner prospects will be obvious by their giving frequency and amount. These names make up your initial working list of donors you'll invite to be monthly partners.

As a team, review the remaining names, alphabetically, by asking these questions that can reveal additional prospects you can invite to join the program:

Which of us, around the table, knows someone who has:

- volunteered during the past year
- corresponded with the organization
- offered an idea
- shared a concern

- networked with staff or leadership
- attended one of our special events
- used their work role or community involvement to further our mission
- been an ambassador of good will
- referred anyone who has become an employee, donor, volunteer or key contact
- shown a desire to become more involved
- expressed a frustration or complaint (that could mask a desire to care and, perhaps, become involved)

The team discussion could surprise you, as you identify individuals and families you may never otherwise have considered to be monthly partner donors. Add their names to the list of people you will invite to launch the Monthly Partner Program.

2. Create the invitation letter and response device

Remember the times in life when you felt chosen, included and accepted? That feeling of being appreciated, valued and important is what you want every person, every monthly partner prospect, to experience. And they *will* through a personable, well-written invitation letter that connects your organization's documented need and vision with a donor's desire to keep supporting life-changing results.

It's important to note the distinction between two invitation letters.

The first letter is an "honor them in" letter you will write to your current core donors who qualify by virtue of the amount and frequency of their giving, plus any helpful psychographic data.

The second letter is a "new prospect" letter which you will send to those outside your current donor base. These can include referrals from a variety of sources.

Both the "honor them in" letter and the "new prospect" letter make up the centerpiece of an initial mailing that includes a response device, brochure and return envelope.

There's a wise saying that goes like this: "You only have one chance to make a positive first impression." Here are the essentials for both types of letters to make a stunning first impression with your donors and hopefully boost the participation level in your Monthly Partner Program.

23

In general, both the "honor them in" and "new prospect" letters will be worded similarly. The main difference will be the opening paragraph:

- **The "honor them in" letter** shows appreciation for the donor by highlighting their faithful participation to date. You are inviting them to join an exclusive group who share a passion for your ministry. Thank them for their faithful support of your organization.
- **The "new prospect" letter** uses an attention-getting line that causes the reader to say, "Tell me more."

After the opening paragraph, follow this sequence for *both* letters:

- **Link their support to positive, significant outcomes**. Early in your letter, tell several specific ways your group (through the loyal support of your faithful donors) has made a life-changing difference.
- **Announce the new opportunity**. Show that the ongoing needs of the people your organization serves have created a new opportunity for involvement that can impact deserving lives every day, 365 days a year. Explain how this new opportunity demands the attention and support of "our most loyal supporters." Announce the creation of a select group of people "whose generosity is unrivaled and whose faithfulness is needed more than ever." Give the name of this "insider's group" and briefly tell how the name reflects the "front line" efforts of your organization.

   Be clear that this is not a fund appeal, nor will you be sending them fund appeals. Rather, they will receive a monthly update on how your organization is able to change lives "thanks to the collective generosity of many loyal monthly partners."
- **Make the invitation**. Clearly and succinctly state what you want the donor to do, and include one or more monthly dollar amounts. Explain how the money will be used to further the causes and efforts the donors value.
- **Explain how it works**. Show how easy and convenient it is to say "Yes." This includes indicating a monthly pledge amount on the enclosed response card and mailing it in the enclosed return

24

envelope. Explain that "each month you will receive a monthly update with news and stories of how your gift – and the collective generosity of others – is making a difference."

Don't forget to offer optional ways to give, including a mail-in check, and (as long as your organization offers these services) electronic funds transfer and online giving.

- **Close with a strong, memorable line**. Your closing remark should act like an exclamation point to a powerful, timely invitation. Repeat the importance of the relationship you want to build with the person.
- **Don't forget the "P.S."** Put the most often read part of any letter to work by offering an irresistible tidbit, statistic or quote that grabs the reader's attention and refers them to a key part of the letter.

On the next page is a sample "honor them in" invitation letter:

April 21, 1995

Your Father in
heaven is not
willing that any of
these little ones
should be lost.
        Matt. 18:14

John & Susan Frank
14642 NE 174th St
Woodinville, WA 98072-4649

Dear John and Susan,

Thank you for your faithful support of the hurting and hungry of the Kokomo area. It is gratifying to see how you have cared for those less fortunate than yourself through your gifts to the Kokomo Rescue Mission.

It's because of your past generosity that I am inviting you to become a charter member of our 99 and ONE Club, a caring group of mission friends committed to giving on a regular basis to shelter and feed the poor.

Based on the parable of the lost sheep found in Matthew 18, the 99 and ONE Club aims to rescue lost men, women and children through the feeding and sheltering programs of the Kokomo Rescue Mission.

Membership in the 99 and ONE Club carries benefits including a convenient monthly response form, an invitation to a special event for club members only and membership materials. You will receive only one mailing each month with your receipt and monthly update in addition to our newsletter.

Will you join with the other club members who make a difference in the lives of the needy of Kokomo? Whether you decide upon a $15, $25 or $100 monthly pledge, your gift will be gratefully received and put to good use. Please use the enclosed reponse card and envelope for your reply.

Thank you for prayerfully considering my invitation to join the 99 and ONE Club. I hope to hear from you soon.

With heartfelt thanks,

Robert M. Cox, Executive Director

Kokomo Rescue Mission
300 W. Mulberry
P.O. Box 476
Kokomo, IN
46903-0476

The response device should be as simple as possible. Remember, "less is more." Research has shown that a lot of print and a multitude of check boxes will scare donors away. Here are the items you need for your response card:

- Name
- Address, City, State, Zip
- Phone – home/work
- Email address
- Desired monthly amount, with suggested tiers
- Request for Electronic Funds Transfer
- Brief instructions for online giving.

Here is a sample of a response device:

Kokomo Rescue Mission
300 W. Mulberry
P.O. Box 476
Kokomo, IN
46903-0476

Please enclose your gift and this form in the envelope provided.

Yes, I accept your invitation to join the 99 and ONE Club, helping the hurting and hungry of our community.

Here is my first monthly pledge gift of:
❑ $15   ❑ $25   ❑ $50   ❑ $100   ❑ Other_____
(Be assured you may cancel your pledge at any time.)

Name _____
Address _____
City _____ State_____ Zip_____
Telephone number (   ) _____
Your number will not be used for telemarketing.

3. Produce the brochure

A simple two-fold, three-panel brochure on your Monthly Partner Program is a nice way to show the benefits to your prospective participants. Here are few simple tips to guide you:

Make the message simple and positive.

On the cover, include you program name, key line, graphic and organization name.

Inside the brochure include a short overview, with five to seven bullet points addressing both the benefits to the monthly partner and the benefits to the organization.

Benefits to the monthly partner:

- Provides a convenient way to give to your favorite organization
- Assures you are making a difference on a consistent basis
- Reaffirms you are adding to the overall strength of the organization

Benefits to the organization:

- Provides consistent cash flow
- Creates a group of ongoing, consistent donors

Include high-quality photos of the audience your organization serves to add to the overall appeal and effectiveness of the piece.

On the back cover include a contact name, phone/fax number, web site and email.

Keep the layout clean. Use a card stock pastel sheet and one- or two-color ink for a quality look that's not splashy or slick. The last thing you want to do is make your brochure a four-color catalog on glossy paper that makes donors wonder why they're supporting a huge printing bill.

See Chapter Ten for samples of two Monthly Partner Program brochures.

Pre-address the return envelope. Pre-paid postage is optional, depending on your budget.

It is always encouraging to begin the monthly partner program with a good start. One client sent out its first invitation to join and about 45 donors joined the program. While this may seem small or large to you, based on your situation, to them in was a good start. Immediately this group of faithful donors began giving on a regular basis. Then they began to recruit other club members. They began to use their brochure in a variety of situations and saw more people join.

Now the fun begins. Who is going to create the letter, produce the brochure and response device, and secure the return and carrier envelopes? Down the hall, in the next room, the answer is closer than you think. . . .

Action Items:
To make this chapter count toward your Monthly Partner Program:
1. Create the list of monthly partners to "honor in" to your program.
2. Create the list of donors you will invite to join your program.
3. Write both the "honor them in" and "new prospect" letters.
4. Write, design and produce your brochure.
5. Write, design and produce your response device.

Chapter Five
The Management System

W hat's wrong with this picture:
My wife Susan and I are monthly partners for several different nonprofit organizations. Every month we receive a reminder letter from each group. Most arrive the last two weeks of the month and, as they do, Susan puts them in the "bills to pay" file. Then regularly on the first Monday of the month she sits down at her desk and writes the checks. We're grateful to support these worthy groups. Yet, we're perplexed by something that, unfortunately, happens all too often.

Susan and I lead busy lives. While I'm on the road, she keeps a full schedule of commitments and friendships. She pays bills only at the first of each month, so if an organization mails us a reminder letter and response envelope by the first of each month we send them a check. Sometimes, however, an organization lags behind and doesn't mail their reminder letter until the middle of the month, after Susan has written the checks. Since we have a check-writing system that works – and we don't have the time to adjust our scheduling commitments to accommodate every organization's letter – we simply put all "late mail" in next month's file.

Susan and I tend to be the exception. While we make up on last month's unpaid pledge, research shows that most people simply do not catch up on missed pledge payments. They don't go back to their records to see what pledge donation they've missed. So, if your monthly mailing arrives in your donors' mailboxes after the first week of the month when most people write their checks, you risk losing that month's donation.

Now, suppose you're the president of one of these "late" organizations. Suppose the same monthly reminder arrives late not only to the Frank family but also to 100, 200, 500 or more monthly partners whose support you need to meet your monthly budget. Now, if the average monthly gift is say, $40, and your letter isn't arriving close to, or on the first, of each month (when most people write their checks), your organization is delaying monthly revenue of $4,000, $8,000, $20,000 or

$40,000 for two, three or more weeks. (And we're not even talking about how a late-arriving monthly letter can weaken the relationship you're trying to build with hundreds, if not thousands, of loyal donors. Much worse, if you *neglect* to send out your monthly reminder, well, that's another story.)

Question: Would you tweak your monthly partner delivery schedule to coincide with the first of each month if you knew it could accelerate your monthly revenue and ensure your donors' faithful generosity? Of course you would. If your goal is to create an effective Monthly Partner Program, wouldn't you like to avoid such costly problems altogether? Absolutely.

Here's the point: While the *impact* of your Monthly Partner Program is felt each time a donor fulfills his monthly pledge, keep in mind your program's ultimate *success* is determined by the sound management system you build in advance.

You can have the best intentions to keep your monthly partners informed, you can write the most compelling letter, your group can even demonstrate the greatest aspirations to serve homeless people, missionaries, adoptive parents or young students. You can do all this, yet your efforts will be for naught without an efficient management system.

In this chapter you're going to learn the three foundational pillars of your management system – and how to maximize the efficiency and complementary strengths of your team.

Three "P's" – Three Keys

I remember the day I visited a client organization with 40 partners. The executive director greeted me warmly in his office. "I can't say enough about the response we're getting from our new Monthly Partner Program," he said. "You won't believe some of the letters we're getting from donors." While I was all ears to hear, my client had something else on his mind.

"John, do you have a minute? You know all about our monthly mailings because you helped us create them. There's something you haven't seen. Come with me." We walked down a hallway and as he led me into a quiet, immaculately organized room the director glanced at me, smiled and said, "This is where it all happens. *This* is what makes our monthly partner program work. . . ."

I stepped into a room where I saw the three keys to an effective management system: *a plan*, efficiently run by capable *people* executing a *production timetable*. Here's what you need to know about each of these three:

The Plan

To run your management system, you will:

1. Produce a monthly reminder package, including:
   a. Letter
   b. Two-part response form
   c. Return envelope
2. Select the monthly partner members from current mailing list
3. Merge letter with list/type letter
4. Mail reminder package to monthly partner list
5. Produce and mail a three-part receipt to each donor
6. Prepare next month's monthly reminder mailing

We'll examine the details of this monthly sequence/cycle in a moment. While some organizations modify the sequence to fit specific needs, these six items don't change because they work for virtually every Monthly Partner Program, including yours.

Your People

Your staff is the second key to your management plan. Basically you need two people with distinctive, complementary skills:

The first person needs to be an *administrator*. He or she is an organizer and planner who thinks sequentially, who knows what needs to get done by what date and who can motivate the necessary people and marshal the needed resources to get the job done.

This person is indispensable for seeing that all of the above steps are completed on time. The good news is that he or she may already be in your midst.

Along with an organizer/planner, you need a *communicator/ambassador*. This person's chief role is to write the appeal letters and advise if not direct the overall creative effort for the Monthly Partner Program. This person can play a key role as an up-front presenter to host special donor events and network with vendors and volunteers involved in your program.

I remember one client who had the perfect administrator and communicator managing their Monthly Partner Program. This tremendous twosome worked together and complemented each other's temperaments and talents. Individually, each was so energized by her own assignments that neither had the time (much less the desire) to interfere with the other's work.

Production Timetable

A workable production timetable is the third key to your management system. This allows your people to work the plan. (For a suggested production timetable, see Chapter Ten.)

Here is a closer look at that plan, broken out in six practical steps:

Step 1.   Produce monthly reminder

These three items create the centerpiece of your campaign:

The reminder letter, as previously noted, is a one-page, two-sided message from the director or president, who thanks the monthly donor for his or her ongoing support. Through one or more testimonial stories, the donor sees the life-changing impact of his or her monthly gift.

The two-part response form offers the donor a convenient way to record each monthly gift with a receipt. The donor sends the organization's copy in . . .

. . . *a pre-addressed, postage-paid return envelope.* Printing these standard-sized envelopes in large quantities can save your organization money.

Step 2.   Select the monthly partner names from current mailing list

Consult your information specialist or the staff person who manages your data base for the most efficient way to secure and manage your names. Once you secure the needed data for your monthly partners, you can computerize the list. Most database software programs include a pledge management program which you can test to make sure it has the proper fields you need for tracking partners. One client's program had a field labeled "arrears" for partners who were not current with their pledge fulfillment. Imagine the embarrassment my client felt when he received less than pleasant phone calls and emails from donors whose reminder letters referred to them by this affectionate term.

Step 3. Merge letter with list/type letter

Your administrative support staff can complete this key step. If your mailing list is small, your director's handwritten signature can add a highly personal touch.

Step 4. Mail the reminder package to the monthly partner list

One of the best things you can do to ensure the success of your Monthly Partner Program is to mail your reminder updates on a consistent, regular schedule so your piece "drops" (that is, received by the donor) on or near the first of each month. Donors today are so swamped with information and preoccupied with the busyness of their own lives that they simply do not remember your organization every waking day. It's unrealistic to expect them to mail in their pledge every 30 days. Your proactive monthly reminder helps them be consistent and fulfill their desire to support you. That's why they joined you in the first place!

To help ensure your monthly partners received your monthly update mailings on time, use this helpful mailing schedule:

MONTHLY PLEDGE UPDATE/RECEIPT MAILING SCHEDULE

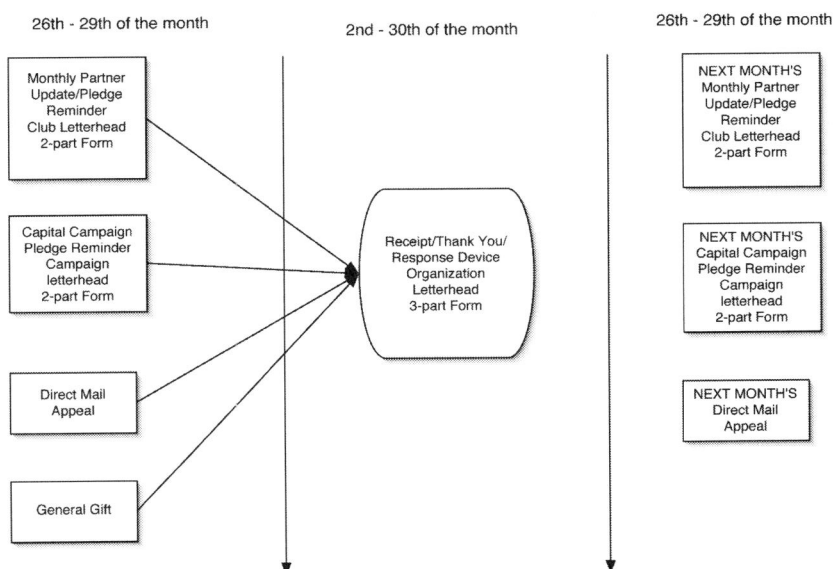

26th - 29th of the month   2nd - 30th of the month   26th - 29th of the month

Monthly Partner Update/Pledge Reminder Club Letterhead 2-part Form

Capital Campaign Pledge Reminder Campaign letterhead 2-part Form

Direct Mail Appeal

General Gift

Receipt/Thank You/ Response Device Organization Letterhead 3-part Form

NEXT MONTH'S Monthly Partner Update/Pledge Reminder Club Letterhead 2-part Form

NEXT MONTH'S Capital Campaign Pledge Reminder Campaign letterhead 2-part Form

NEXT MONTH'S Direct Mail Appeal

33

Step 5. Produce and mail a three-part receipt to each donor

Follow along with me carefully, because this is one of the most important elements of your entire program: *Within two days of receiving each monthly partner gift, mail a three-part receipt to the donor.*

Use the organization's letterhead – *not* the Monthly Partner Program's letterhead. Remember, the donor's gift supports the work of the organization, not the operational efforts of the program.

A common question from leaders is, "Why do we need a separate mailing for the receipt? Why can't we just include the receipt with the next month's reminder letter?" The answer is that every effective Monthly Partner Program relies on a clockwork operation that systematically mails out a new reminder letter every 30 days.

To build and ensure a trusting relationship with each donor, you need to send a receipt within two to seven days, and that means a separate, responsive approach apart from the established cycle of monthly reminders. Therefore, forcing the donor to wait several weeks just so you can include the receipt with the next month's reminder letter is unacceptable.

Step 6. Prepare next month's monthly reminder mailing

Within 20 days of mailing your monthly reminder, you will need to create the next month's letter and repeat the six-step cycle. Most organizations develop a familiarity with the sequence within two or three months. The front-end investment of time and effort pays off in the long run, as you reap the efficiencies of people who can execute their clearly defined tasks within a workable timetable.

Creating your management system is much like helping a homeless person move into a new apartment for the first time. There's a lot to set up, a lot to do, a lot to coordinate. But, once you get established, the ongoing management becomes a regular way of life.

With a proven plan and skilled people committed to a doable production timetable you can create an effective management system, a system that will launch your Monthly Partner Program and ensure its effectiveness for nurturing solid donor relationships for months and years to come.

Action Items

To make this chapter count toward a Monthly Partner Program:

1. Complete the six steps of the plan.
2. Make sure your people are in place.
3. Use the examples in this chapter, as well as those in Chapter Ten, to create your own production timetable.

Chapter Six

The Monthly Reminder/Update & Response Device

You know your Monthly Partner Program is working when your donors view it as a lifetime membership in a very desirable club. Your organization's *invitation letter* – both the "honor them in" and the "new prospect" versions – acts like a virtual "open house" that encourages people to look around at a place they can call their own.

Your *monthly reminder/update* reaffirms the decision to join – and reinforces the constant desire to belong.

In this chapter we want to look at why the monthly reminder is important, as well as produce an update letter and accompanying response device that can solidify and even grow your monthly partner program.

Not an appeal but an update

Virtually every leader I've introduced to the Monthly Partner Program approach (including some who became clients) views it through the lens of regular fund appeals. Such appeals come from every group under the sun and have permanently colored the way we view and even read our own mail.

Whatever bias you have toward regular fund appeals, or direct mail for that matter, consider how the distinct advantages of the monthly reminder keeps your loyal monthly partners informed, motivated and engaged:

A fund appeal asks the recipient to give.

The monthly reminder thanks the donor for his or her consistent giving.

A fund appeal shows the benefits of "what your gift will mean."

The monthly reminder thanks the donor for "how your gift is now at work transforming lives."

A fund appeal uses urgency to motivate a one-time response.

The monthly reminder relies on compelling life stories to reaffirm a donor's continuing relationship as a monthly partner.

A fund appeal offers a donor books, pendants and other gift premiums to stimulate giving.

The monthly reminder offers a donor the priceless satisfaction of one's ongoing generosity.

A fund appeal "never stops selling."

The monthly reminder never ceases to honor the generosity of every donor, whatever the size of the gift.

Bottom line: The monthly update reminds your donors of the commitment they've already made to your organization. It is a reminder to a friend. The tone is warm, the message clear: "We greatly value our relationship with you and your unflagging support."

To lose sight of this ongoing word of thanks, switch tracks and ask your monthly partners to give would be inconsiderate of their expressed earlier commitment. It would be like asking one of your loyal volunteers to give of their time when he or she has already said, "Yes, I'll be there. You can count on me."

Here are two basics for producing your monthly reminder/update letter and accompanying response device:

Engaging content, appealing warmth

The update letter, below, honors and affirms faithful donors. Read the letter; see if you can identify at least six reasons it's so effective:

Dear Bill and Mary,

The other day I was speaking with one of our staff who works with the children. They shared this story with me and I thought you would want to hear it.

One of the children new to our organization has come from a tough situation. For most of the first two weeks she would not smile or talk to anyone. Then at bedtime prayers the other day, she looked up at our staff person, smiled, and said she felt safe for the first time in her life.

As you can imagine, this was a very moving moment to all of us. And this happens because of you. Your prayers and faithful support make this possible.

Thank you again for standing with us every month for the children. I want you to know how important you are. Every day there is the potential for a breakthrough with these children.

Thank you and may God bless you,

(Signed, organization's director)

Write down the winning qualities of this letter and see how your observations match up to strengths you'll want in your reminder letters. . . .

The organization's monthly update includes these six benchmarks of strong content and effective layout:

- *The opening sentence* is immediately engaging.
- *The friendly tone* and repeated use of "you" makes the donor feel the director is writing to the recipient alone. (Notice the absence of impersonal phrases like "all of our faithful partners," that suggest the director is writing to a group.)
- *The testimonial* is compelling. It has all the makings of a good story: a *beginning* that grabs your attention, a *middle* that reveals an unfolding predicament of need that makes you say, "Tell me more," and an *ending* that shows how a person's life is better because of the organization's involvement.
- *The close* of the letter reaffirms the director's appreciation for the donor and donor's relationship with the organization.
- *A personal, handwritten signature* is a wonderful, personal touch. Your director will also score big points with your donors by writing a personal line at the bottom of the letter – "Good to see you the other day," or "I appreciate you!"

Timely news

Your update letter can carry added weight if your Monthly Partner Program is focused on a specific project.

You can increase the likelihood that donors will read your letter by incorporating these six "update" items:

- *Always remind your monthly partners of your project's purpose.* Your donors are busy people and need a quick, ten-second reminder of what they're helping your organization accomplish.
- *If appropriate, make the progress of your program measurable,* such as the increase in the number of people being helped, affected or served.
- *Use a graph* to clearly show the impact of your project on your audience.

- *Remind your monthly partners of the important work that remains to be done*, the ongoing needs "your generous gifts are helping to meet."
- *Include a "zinger" quote* from a person whose life has been touched, recently, by the project. Such a candid, positive remark can create fresh, new immediacy with your monthly partners.
- *Be date sensitive.* The name "monthly partners" is a literal reminder to your organization that your donors look forward to hearing from you at a given time each month. This is especially true if your project has date sensitive matter, such as an event tie-in, or any calendar-related item that's part of your organization's ongoing effort to serve others.

The monthly response device

This simple "tear-off" form gives your donors a helpful way to track their monthly giving. The reminder letter and response device are actually two elements that fit on a single sheet. The top section is the letter, the bottom section is the response device that the donor tears off and mails back to your organization with the monthly check. A two-part carbonless receipt is suggested, since it provides the donor with both the mail-back form and a receipt to keep in home files.

Design your monthly response device to include this basic information:

- Donor's name
- Monthly pledge amount
- Total monthly partner gifts – year to date
- Other gifts
- Total gifts included

On the following page is a sample of a monthly reminder/update letter:

"Rejoice with Me for I have
found My lost sheep." Luke 15:6

Rev. Herbert A. Pfiffner
Executive Director

11/20/92

Dear John and Susan,

As we move into this busy time of year, I've become especially aware of all the hungry people who come to us asking for food. Their needs are immense.

I've seen long lines of men, women and families grateful to wait, often in the rain, for one of the 1,200 meals we serve at our Men's Shelter. I see dozens of hungry kids at our Reach Out Youth Center crowding the tables, eager to dive into plates of spaghetti prepared for them by volunteers.

At our Women and Family Shelter, up to 75 homeless women and parents with children gratefully sit down to hot and nutritious meals. Three times a day, the men in our New Vision drug and alcohol recovery program sit down in the dining room at the Son Shine Inn to eat and have fellowship.

I am so thankful for your partnership with us through both the 99 & One club and your pledge for our Continuing the Vision campaign. Your continued pledge support is critical as we complete the capital projects to upgrade our facilities.

Thank you so much for your faithful help in this work, which enables us to offer hot meals, shelter and assistance to these hungry and needy people.

The Lord bless and keep you,

Herbert A. Pfiffner
Executive Director

Union Gospel Mission • PO Box 202 • Seattle, WA 98111-0202 • (206) 723-0767

Pledge Gift Response Form

"Rejoice with Me for I have
found My lost sheep." Luke 15:6

PO Box 202
Seattle, WA 98111-0202
(206) 723-0767

FRAN14800

Please make your checks payable to Union Gospel Mission. We will send you a receipt. Thank you!

Mr. and Mrs. John R. Frank
14800 - 127th Ave. N.E.
Kirkland, WA 98034

For the month of December

99 & ONE Club
Pledge-Monthly $ 30.00
1992-99&ONE Gifts $ 240.00

Continuing the Vision
Capital Campaign
Pledge-Monthly $ 30.00
Total Campaign Gifts $ 945.00

****
Total 1992-All Gifts $ 585.00

AMOUNT ENCLOSED $_____

Please write any prayer request you may have on back.
Our staff will be praying for you!

41

Some organizations use a coupon book mailed to each donor when he or she becomes a monthly partner. Each month, the donor tears off that month's coupon and includes it with the monthly check. A coupon book can be an effective "silent reminder" to donors who have developed a consistent pattern of writing their monthly checks.

The goal of this streamlined list is to help you avoid mailing additional letters about outstanding pledges. Donors can do the math to see their monthly commitment in light of their year-to-date total. Such an approach shows respect for the faithful donors and keeps them informed of their giving history.

An important feature of the monthly partner response device is a simple line you include at the bottom of the form:

Please put your prayer requests on the back of this form and our staff will be praying for you.

Here is a sample of how one organization invites monthly partners to send in their prayer requests:

Thank you for your faithful support of Portland Rescue Mission.
Your gift is tax-deductible to the full extent of the law. We will send a receipt for your records.

❏ I would like to receive information about the Mission via email whenever possible.

My email address is: _____
(example: yourname@serviceprovider.com, please print)

❏ I am interested in receiving general information on estate planning and the tax benefits of charitable gifts.

❏ Please pray for:

It's amazing how this personal request touches donors.

In helping one client organization, we created postcards with the partner program logo. When prayer requests came in, we gave the cards to staff members who volunteered to pray and then write to the partner.

One staff member prayed for a donor's father who had cancer. Another prayed for the spiritual situation that a member was experiencing. Still another prayed about a member's family crisis.

By inviting donors to share their prayer requests an organization shows it is serious about building a caring relationship with its monthly partners. You show that while money is important, the well-being of those in your giving family is close to your heart. After all, your donors are people. They have real needs and view your organization as part of their lives. In some cases they look upon you as part of their family.

See your monthly reminder letter and accompanying response device for what they are, a personal, convenient means for your donors to make good on their pledge to give regularly to your organization.

Against the backdrop of noisy fund appeals, your monthly reminders will bring a sigh of relief to your monthly partners. For once an organization they believe in isn't asking them to give, give, give. Not when they can see where their dollars are already making a difference.

That's a great feeling for your donors who will be there for you month after month – and good news for any organization that cherishes such priceless, ongoing relationships.

Action Items:

To make this chapter count toward a Monthly Partner Program:

1. Word your monthly reminder letter as if you were writing to a friend.
2. Find an effective way to capture testimonial stories and anecdotes for your monthly reminder letters. This may include using key frontline contacts, phone calls, and involving a point person, such as your program director.
3. Create a monthly response device compatible with your computer system and consistent in look and feel with your donors.

Chapter Seven

The Gift of Appreciation

Imagine inviting all of your monthly partners to a special open house at your organization's headquarters. Scores of people come through the front door. Each and every one is personally greeted by your director. To a person, each one feels special. Many say it is the most memorable event they've ever attended. In the next day's mail, your organization receives a $2,500 check from a donor who is so impressed by the work of the organization that he and his wife are increasing their monthly partner gift from $200 to $500.

This true story demonstrates what can happen when you take time to thank your loyal donors. Whether it's a special event or a gift-wrapped item, a single expression of appreciation on behalf of your organization can propel the valued relationships with your monthly partners to a new level.

In this chapter, you are going to see three simple ways to deepen the trust and goodwill between you and your monthly partners

The unexpected annual gift

You can send each of your loyal donors a special gift of appreciation. I know a number of nonprofit organizations that do this. Somewhere between Thanksgiving and Christmas they send a thank-you gift to each of their monthly partners. What appears at first blush as a simple, inexpensive item becomes a noteworthy gesture of appreciation to individuals and families, singles and couples, young professionals and retirees. All realize the organization they continue to support monthly really does take the time to say "Thank you!"

One client of mine decided to send a small gift card with a laminated angel. The response from their donors was very positive.

Gifts of appreciation can include a bookmark, paperweight, calendar, pen, notepad or key chain. It's important to match the appreciation gift to your donors. As a rule, you neither want to be too flashy nor too frugal with a gift, which can be classy without breaking the bank.

Another organization sent each of its monthly partners a paper memo cube with the Monthly Partner Program name and logo printed on the side. As donors used the memo cube at their desks or kitchen phone nooks they were reminded of the club. Donors considered the memo cube a quality, practical little tool for a phone number, driving directions or shopping list. In fact, it was so effective the group renewed it annually for several more years.

What made each of these gifts appropriate and meaningful was that they were in keeping, both in style and expense, with their respective donors.

Your gifts should be consistent with who you are as an organization. Something "off the wall" can cause donors to believe their financial support has been wasted on cheap trinkets, or "extras." Remember, many monthly partners give modest amounts. Therefore, they may respond most favorably to a modest gift that helps them see the organization's intent; the spirit of appreciation behind the gift is just as important as the item itself.

Your gift of appreciation is separate from your monthly reminder. When sending a gift, do not include a reminder/update or a response device, only a brief note of thanks for the donor's faithful support.

Special events that live up to their name

Monthly partners, like people everywhere, long to be part of something bigger than themselves. Certainly, they act upon this desire as they give themselves to your organization and see their hopes and dreams, values and faith, expressed in the testimonials they read in your monthly reminders.

Yet, if you want to see your donors' eyes really light up, if you want to draw them ever closer to the organization, nothing can take the place of a face-to-face opportunity to meet with your director and staff in a special event with the unabashed purpose of honoring each and every monthly partner.

At a special event, your monthly partners can experience, first hand, the people who make your organization run. Based upon how you create your special event, your donors may even meet some of the people your organization serves. In these persons, they can see how their monthly gifts are making a life-changing impact.

The organization I referred to at the start of this chapter produced a fabulous open house. The leadership of this rescue mission knew they could touch the hearts and stir the minds of their donors by inviting them to their urban ministry headquarters where these faithful givers could get a firsthand glimpse of the mission's passion and purpose.

Here are just some of the many things the event's organizers did right:

- Board members sat at each table, so that each donor would be made to feel special and more connected to the organization.
- On each table were copies of the current newsletter featuring a homeless man being served by the mission.
- A very tasteful PowerPoint presentation showed current photos of the mission's homeless clientele – including the man featured in the newsletter. While donors saw these pictures, they were treated to a moving song performed live by a local singer.
- This creative combination of music, spoken word and visuals drove home a compelling message to donors: "With your help, we can break the cycle of homelessness."
- The highlight of the event came when each donor was called by name and asked to come forward to receive a special commemorative plate, as the organization's staff applauded. And, yet there was still more.
- After the donors received their plates, room partitions were pulled back to reveal a men's chorus – made up entirely of homeless men served by the mission – who sang to honor the donors.

Another way to host a reception is to hold a "monthly partners only" get-together before the organization's annual banquet. You can set up a nearby room where donors can meet your director, leadership team and staff. To make the gathering truly memorable, you can arrange to have the banquet speaker meet the donors. Imagine the look on your donors' faces when you hand each an autographed copy of the speaker's book or CD.

If your organization has a site or facility conducive to tours, a "monthly partners only" open house can give your donors an inside look at your operation. This can work well if you have multiple facilities. Your tour may start with a light lunch at one site, followed by a short bus ride to other nearby facilities. You can do a progressive dessert, eating, meeting and greeting as you go.

A short welcome, a word from your director (ideally) or other senior leadership, and a question-and-answer time are nice ways to tell your organization's story and giving donors a worthwhile time. An open house allows monthly partners to bring family members and friends, who can learn about your organization through printed materials, CDs and tapes you make available. Who knows, they may decide to become monthly partners themselves!

Prayer

Earlier, we saw how a simple invitation at the bottom of each monthly response card can help create a meaningful prayer relationship between your staff and your donors.

Talk about a demonstrated way to draw your loyal monthly donors ever closer to the heart of your ministry! Creating a prayer partnership between you and your dedicated followers will provide strength, support and long-term commitment to your Monthly Partner Program.

Appreciation expressed in many ways

An annual gift brings unexpected blessing to the doorstep of every monthly donor.

A special event fulfills the desire of each monthly partner to be recognized, in person, by your leadership.

An invitation to all donors with every monthly reminder to share a personal prayer request demonstrates that the organization they support is serious about building and maintaining a meaningful relationship.

All of these things add up to a gift of appreciation that touches the hearts and minds of your monthly partners. And once a year, the best opportunity of all awaits. . . .

Action Items:

To make this chapter count toward a Monthly Partner Program:

1. Think of an appropriate annual appreciation gift for your monthly partners.
2. If appropriate, design a special event for your monthly partners.
3. Create a simple invitation for prayer requests that both honors God and involves your donors.

Chapter Eight

The Inseparable Bond

To this point, we have focused on building your Monthly Partner Program. Once your program is off the ground, how do you keep it flying? How can you be the best possible steward of your time, energy and resources to sustain and grow this important fundraising effort?

In this chapter, you are going to learn five ways to retain your monthly partners, increase their number and enhance your long-term relationship with them.

Annual Invitation Letter

Your Monthly Partner Program fulfills your donors' desire to belong to a group of like-minded people. Your donors will appreciate being part of an insider's club, not because it excludes others but because it makes them feel included, important and valued.

You launch your Monthly Partner Program by taking the initiative to invite your donors to join.

You can *grow* your monthly partner program the same way, by being proactive and mailing an annual invitation letter to *a new list of monthly partner prospects*. Even before you launch your program, it is wise to realize where you are likely to find new partner-members. These include:

- donors who did not say "Yes" to your initial invitation
- newly acquired donors (secured during the 12 months after your launch)
- donors whose increased annual giving "bumped them up" from "impulse donor" to "core donor," and
- referrals from initial monthly partner members

The best time to mail your annual invitation letter is either in January or September. January is advantageous because many people like to get off to a fresh start in the new year. They're ready to make new commitments. Because it marks the start of the school year, September is a good time to invite people to join. Families, in particular, regroup in September, and they're more ready than in spring, summer or late fall to make a new commitment.

How do you reach these new prospects? What should your mailing include? The essential items are virtually identical to those in the initial invitation packet:

- Invitation letter from the director
- Monthly Partner Program brochure
- Response device
- Return envelope
- General brochure and newsletter (optional)

Newsletter

Your organization's newsletter is an excellent way to generate new monthly partners. This is not an advertisement that tries to sell people on anything. Rather, it is a gentle wake-up kind of piece that causes people to say, "I didn't know about this. Tell me more. . ."

Once or twice a year, write an article that reports on the positive developments of the program. An informative article that motivates and encourages readers to join should include news about:

- the program's initial appeal and numeric growth
- one or more monthly partners – why they joined and what keeps them fulfilled
- how Monthly Partner Program funds are making a life-changing difference
- upcoming monthly partner events "open to all"
- Phone number, email and web site "for more information and to join!"
- Optional: Include the name of the staff person or recruitment co-ordinator best prepared to respond to phone calls and emails. This will reinforce the personal approach, create a strong first impression and build relationships, so vital in the Monthly Partner Program.

If your newsletter has limited space, focus on "the big three" – *what* the program is all about, *who* it helps and *how* you can belong. *Always* include a phone number and any appropriate ways people can contact your organization to become a monthly partner.

Today, the Internet and emailed attachments allow you to distribute an electronic newsletter at less cost than a traditional publication. By including a check box option on your monthly response device, your donors can specify if they would like to receive your organization's newsletter online. You can also post a separate web page, exclusively for your monthly partners.

Special Event Banquet

When it comes to your Monthly Partner Program, an annual banquet can be effective on several levels. For instance, you can:

- ask a donor to share a brief, three-minute testimony on what he or she finds most fulfilling as a monthly partner
- involve a recipient of your organization's services, whose life-changing story offers powerful evidence of your group's work – and helps set up "the ask"
- invite banquet attendees into the Monthly Partner Program, as one of several options for giving to your organization

Electronic Funds Transfer

It's called EFT, and it's quickly becoming one of the most popular means donors are choosing to give to their charities of choice. Today, people use EFT to pay their home mortgage, utility and gas bills, and car payments.

Announcing that your organization offers EFT will alert your monthly partner donors, particularly tech-savvy busters, to this time-saving convenience. Electronic funds transfer is one more way you can serve *all* of your donors in their giving, stewardship and philanthropy.

The benefits of EFT for your organization are enormous, including consistent cash flow you can count on month after month. Plus, EFT donors tend to maintain a consistent giving pattern, since there is no "pre-programmed alarm" in their bank's computer system to tell the donor it's time to re-up as a monthly partner.

Your organization's web site is the logical way for donors to sign up for electronic funds transfer. Consult your information technology specialist or webmaster.

Web Site

Your organization's web site is the logical way for some donors (see "Busters," Chapter Three) to sign up to become monthly partners. They can give single or monthly gifts through your web site. To be even more effective, create a separate page for your monthly partner members. Such a page could offer more in-depth stories, information on EFT, or an upcoming monthly partner event.

Challenge Letter

Because monthly partners are some of your most committed donors, there may be appropriate times to offer them a challenge to give "over and above" their current financial commitment.

Such a challenge can respond to a financial crisis or a special project. One of my clients encountered a pesky bark beetle at a camp in California. Thousands of these nasty insects threatened to eat their way through the facilities. The camp was forced to cut down hundreds of trees. The director sent an urgent, one-time invitation asking faithful donors for funds to cut down the trees and stop the bark beetle's devastation. Generous donors responded with $100,000.

Keep in mind:

- Do not position the letter as a fund appeal. Do not try a new strategy to double dip. This does not honor their faithful support, nor does it have a place in a successful challenge opportunity. Stay true to the principle, described earlier, that your monthly donors have already chosen to support your organization. You don't need to sell them on your group. Rather, invite them to extend their loyal involvement to meet an unforeseen need.
- If you can hold on and address your urgent need until after the first of the year, January can be a strategic time to challenge your monthly donors. If you're like some nonprofit groups, the start of the year can be a slow time, financially, and a one-time donation from your monthly partners can help meet your specific need. The donations can also provide a huge psychological lift to your staff and leadership trying to get their feet on the ground and establish some traction after the first of the year.
- Conventional wisdom says, "Our donors are already giving. Let's not bother them with a special request for funds." How-

ever, there's another side to this issue: By *not* sending out a challenge letter to meet a bona fide need – and shutting down a program element because of lack of funds – how would you answer donors who say, "Why didn't I know about this? I would have contributed to this special need – if only I had known."

Your annual invitation, newsletter, annual events, electronic funds transfer and special one-time challenges offer you specific opportunities to reach and serve some wonderful individuals who would love to support your organization on a monthly basis – if only they knew how.

Another true story: One of my clients received $13,400 in monthly giving from their monthly partners. A year later their Monthly Partner Program income increased 28 percent to $17,200. The number of monthly gifts went from 249 to 584 in two years. And their yearly monthly partner income jumped from $118,500 to $151,418.

None of these increases took place overnight. The growing generosity of this group's monthly partners was the result of the organization doing everything they could to value the relationship with their donors – from taking the time to add individual handwritten thank-you notes to delivering special appreciation gifts to the homes of their member-partners. Do everything you can to value your relationship with your monthly partners. Find a way to involve and thank your donors. Do it in a way that draws them ever closer to the work of your organization. See these acts not as a monthly task but as ongoing expressions of your organization's heart and soul. Do these things and you will build an inseparable bond with donors – for life.

Action Items:
To make this chapter count toward a Monthly Partner Program:
1. Identify and prioritize the opportunities mentioned in this chapter – annual invitation letter, newsletter, special event banquet, electronic funds transfer and challenge letter – weighing projected costs against anticipated benefits.
2. Swiftly follow through on these decisions.
3. Brainstorm new ways to attract new monthly partners, as well as ask current monthly partners to increase their giving.

PUTTING IT INTO ACTION

The invaluable tools you need to begin

How do you successfully launch your Monthly Partner Program? Chapters Nine and Ten reveal the specific steps and practical communication tools to sign up your member-donors and build your program.

❦

Chapter Nine

The Opportunity Is Now!

One of the most incredible things I've ever witnessed is the sight of an Olympic high diver preparing to jump. This world-class athlete has trained for this single moment. He knows the perfect dive can redefine and culminate his career.

What would happen if the diver suddenly got cold feet, walked away from the edge and refused to dive because he was too nervous, too unsure of himself, too afraid of the outcome?

Maybe you are a leader of a nonprofit organization and the thought of starting a Monthly Partner Program seems like a big leap.

I don't want to dismiss your concerns. Any time you reach out to involve donors, you take a risk. The worst thing that can happen is that someone might say, "No."

Your loyal donors, however, the people who have stood behind you for years and who will continue standing with you for years to come, *will* have something to say about your organization's ultimate impact.

They believe in you.

They trust you.

They want to know their gifts matter.

They know the quality work your organization does. They've read the stories. They've even told others about the great things you're doing.

The time is at hand. The time has come to give your donors what they most want, and that's a new *sense of belonging*, a reaffirmation that they can truly make a difference in the lives and communities your organization is helping to transform.

Your donors want to feel included.

Your donors want to know their giving counts – and they *will* when you invite them to become monthly partners.

The second greatest thing you can offer your donors is the *invitation to join a group of like-minded people* who share their values, their heart and their desire to further the work of your organization.

The greatest thing you can fulfill for each donor who becomes a monthly partner is a deep and lasting relationship with your organization.

Every day, hundreds of monthly partners are assured of the fact their regular gifts are making a difference. These donors know their contributions to an inner city mission in Seattle will mean that homeless men will not go hungry. Nor will they be forced to sleep under bridges or in abandoned cars.

The Monthly Partner Program has helped transform the lives of these once desperate men.

The Monthly Partner Program can transform the impact of your organization. The blueprints are in your hands.

The opportunity is now.

Create your own Monthly Partner Program and you will reap the priceless reward of making your donors feel honored, valued and involved. Such satisfaction and participation is what they desire.

The good news is this: Even before you ask them to join, inside they're already saying "Yes."

Important!

Don't put down this book.

What you do in the next few minutes could make a significant difference in the immediate impact and ultimate effectiveness of your Monthly Partner Program.

Turn the page and see why. . . .

Chapter Ten

Resources for Launching Your Monthly Partner Program

The tools in this chapter offer important guidelines to track your progress. Each is designed to help you maximize your time, talent and resources.

The Action Item Master Checklist gives you the key "next steps," found at the end of each chapter, in one summary list.

The Production Timetable gives you guidelines for how much time you will need to implement these steps in a calendar year.

The Monthly Management Calendar outlines the 30-day sequence/cycle for producing your monthly reminder/update letters.

The sample letters, response devices and brochures give you practical examples to create the important communication pieces for the program.

Action Item Master Checklist

Use this master list to ensure timely follow-through and track the progress of your Monthly Partner Program.

Chapter One
1. Meet with your key leadership to present the monthly partner program.
2. Obtain buy-in and consensus for the program from your leadership.
3. Make the decision to start!

Chapter Two
1. Identify and prioritize the donor benefits of your Monthly Partner Program. (You will articulate these later in your brochure, see Chapter Four).
2. Become familiar with your target segment.
3. List possible projects your Monthly Partner Program can fund.
4. Come up with a program name that reflects the loyalty of your donors and the front-line impact on those your organization serves.

5. Create an implementation calendar with key production deadlines for sending out your monthly reminder. More in Chapter Five).

6. Brainstorm some creative ways you can appeal to the "inner circle" (from among your core donors) and draw them closer to the life-changing impact of your organization.

Chapter Three

1. Find your donors who are currently giving monthly. These are the donors you will "honor in."

2. Do a search of your data base for donors who have given three, four or more times this past year.

3. Identify the builders, boomers and busters among your donor base.

4. Spot demographic, cultural and lifestyle trends in your community that may affect giving to your organization.

Chapter Four

1. Create the list of monthly partners to "honor in" to your program.

2. Create the list of donors you will invite to join your program.

3. Write both the "honor them in" and "new prospect" letters.

4. Write, design and produce your brochure.

5. Write, design and produce your response device.

Chapter Five

1. Complete the six steps of the Plan.

2. Make sure your People are in place.

3. Use the examples in this chapter, as well as those in Chapter Ten, to create your own Production Timetable.

Chapter Six

1. Word your monthly reminder letter as if you were writing to a friend.

2. Find an effective way to capture testimonial stories and anecdotes for your monthly reminder letters. This may include using key front-line contacts, phone calls, and involving a point person, such as your program director.

3. Create a monthly response device compatible with your computer system and consistent in look and feel with your donors.

Chapter Seven

1. Think of an appropriate annual appreciation gift for your monthly partners.

2. If appropriate, design a special event for your monthly partners.

3. Create a simple invitation for prayer requests that both honors God and involves your donors.

Chapter Eight

1. Identify and prioritize the opportunities mentioned in this chapter – annual invitation letter, newsletter, special event banquet, electronic funds transfer and challenge letter – weighing projected costs against anticipated benefits.

2. Swiftly follow through on these decisions.

3. Brainstorm new ways to attract new monthly partners, as well as ask current monthly partners to increase their giving.

Production Timetable

The two best times of the year to launch your Monthly Partner Program are January 1 and September 1. This helpful planning calendar shows you how much time to allow for each needed phase to successfully create your own program:

	Task	Months before Launch date
1.	Determine Monthly Partner Program overall implementation strategy	**12**
2.	Create name	**11**
3.	Design internal management strategy	**10**
4.	Select relationships to be "honored in"	**6**
5.	Select relationships to be invited to join	**3**
6.	Create membership package	**3**
7.	Create invitation package	**2**
8.	Train staff in relationship management	**1**
	JAN. 1/SEPT.1 LAUNCH!	
	Send "honored in" letter	**0**
9.	Send "invitation" letter	**0**
10.	Begin monthly update management	**Feb. 1/Oct. 1**

Monthly Management Calendar

This helpful planning calendar gives you a recommended time frame to complete the necessary steps each month to successfully manage your Monthly Partner Program.

	Task	Date
1.	Write monthly update letter	**7th-10th**
2.	Select members to be updated by mail (EFT/Web excluded unless requested)	**15th**
3.	Merge letter with list and pledge information (provided by database pledge management)	**20th**
4.	Mail monthly reminder/update based on distance	**26th-29th**
5.	Monthly reminder/update received by donor	**1st (of the new month)**
6.	Write monthly thank-you letter to be used in receipt reply	
7.	Send receipt/thank you letter as gifts come in	**Within 72 hours of receiving gift**
8.	Begin planning/writing next month's update letter	

Sample Pieces

Effective communication is central to a successful Monthly Partner Program. The samples on the following pages, taken from successful programs, give you an idea of how to create efficient pieces on a limited budget.

Monthly partner invitation letter
Kokomo Rescue Mission, Kokomo, Ind.

Your Father in heaven is not willing that any of these little ones should be lost.
Matt. 18:14

April 21, 1995

John & Susan Frank
14642 NE 174th St
Woodinville, WA 98072-4649

Dear John and Susan,

Thank you for your faithful support of the hurting and hungry of the Kokomo area. It is gratifying to see how you have cared for those less fortunate than yourself through your gifts to the Kokomo Rescue Mission.

It's because of your past generosity that I am inviting you to become a charter member of our 99 and ONE Club, a caring group of mission friends committed to giving on a regular basis to shelter and feed the poor.

Based on the parable of the lost sheep found in Matthew 18, the 99 and ONE Club aims to rescue lost men, women and children through the feeding and sheltering programs of the Kokomo Rescue Mission.

Membership in the 99 and ONE Club carries benefits including a convenient monthly response form, an invitation to a special event for club members only and membership materials. You will receive only one mailing each month with your receipt and monthly update in addition to our newsletter.

Will you join with the other club members who make a difference in the lives of the needy of Kokomo? Whether you decide upon a $15, $25 or $100 monthly pledge, your gift will be gratefully received and put to good use. Please use the enclosed reponse card and envelope for your reply.

Thank you for prayerfully considering my invitation to join the 99 and ONE Club. I hope to hear from you soon.

With heartfelt thanks,

Robert M. Cox, Executive Director

Kokomo Rescue Mission
300 W. Mulberry
P.O. Box 476
Kokomo, IN
46903-0476

61

Monthly reminder/update letter
Union Gospel Mission, Seattle, Wash.

"Rejoice with Me for I have found My lost sheep." Luke 15:6

11/20/92

Rev. Herbert A. Pfiffner
Executive Director

Dear John and Susan,

As we move into this busy time of year, I've become especially aware of all the hungry people who come to us asking for food. Their needs are immense.

I've seen long lines of men, women and families grateful to wait, often in the rain, for one of the 1,200 meals we serve at our Men's Shelter. I see dozens of hungry kids at our Reach Out Youth Center crowding the tables, eager to dive into plates of spaghetti prepared for them by volunteers.

At our Women and Family Shelter, up to 75 homeless women and parents with children gratefully sit down to hot and nutritious meals. Three times a day, the men in our New Vision drug and alcohol recovery program sit down in the dining room at the Son Shine Inn to eat and have fellowship.

I am so thankful for your partnership with us through both the 99 & One club and your pledge for our Continuing the Vision campaign. Your continued pledge support is critical as we complete the capital projects to upgrade our facilities.

Thank you so much for your faithful help in this work, which enables us to offer hot meals, shelter and assistance to these hungry and needy people.

The Lord bless and keep you,

Herbert A. Pfiffner
Executive Director

Union Gospel Mission • PO Box 202 • Seattle, WA 98111-0202 • (206) 723-0767

"Rejoice with Me for I have found My lost sheep." Luke 15:6

PO Box 202
Seattle, WA 98111-0202
(206) 723-0767

Pledge Gift Response Form

FRAN14800

Please make your checks payable to Union Gospel Mission. We will send you a receipt. Thank you!

Mr. and Mrs. John R. Frank
14800 - 127th Ave. N.E.
Kirkland, WA 98034

For the month of December

99 & ONE Club
Pledge-Monthly $ 30.00
1992-99&ONE Gifts $ 240.00

**Continuing the Vision
Capital Campaign**
Pledge-Monthly $ 30.00
Total Campaign Gifts $ 945.00

****
Total 1992-All Gifts $ 585.00

AMOUNT ENCLOSED $_____

Please write any prayer request you may have on back.
Our staff will be praying for you!

Monthly reminder/update letter, with gift receipt
Portland Rescue Mission, Portland, Ore.

June Reminder

PORTLAND RESCUE MISSION
111 WEST BURNSIDE ST.
PORTLAND, OREGON 97209

May 22, 2002

«AdditSal01»
«AddrL1»
«City», «St» «ZipCd»

Dear «AdditSal02»:

Before I do anything else, I want to tell you what a blessing your support is to us.

Each gift you send not only provides food, shelter and other vital services, but brings the message of God's redeeming love to the Portland area's neediest people!

I hope you feel as much joy as I do at being able to serve the Lord so faithfully!

Thanks to your monthly gifts, here's the work we'll be able to accomplish this summer:

- Feed more than 25,000 hot, nutritious meals to hungry men, women and children.

- Provide over 90 nights of shelter.

- Enable an average of 70 men and women to receive Christian counseling, work training and other vital services.

Your gift is also enabling us to expand our Learning Center and Employment Services.

Without your support, there would be no food for those who are hungry, no shelter for those who are homeless. Those who search for a better life would be in despair!

Please help us continue this vital work by mailing your July monthly gift today. Thank you!

Sincerely,

Michael R. Maksimowicz
Executive Director

P. S. I hope you know how much I value your partnership in this important ministry. God bless you for rushing your gift to help us mend broken lives with His love.

Pledge gift response form (blank)
Union Gospel Mission, Seattle, Wash.

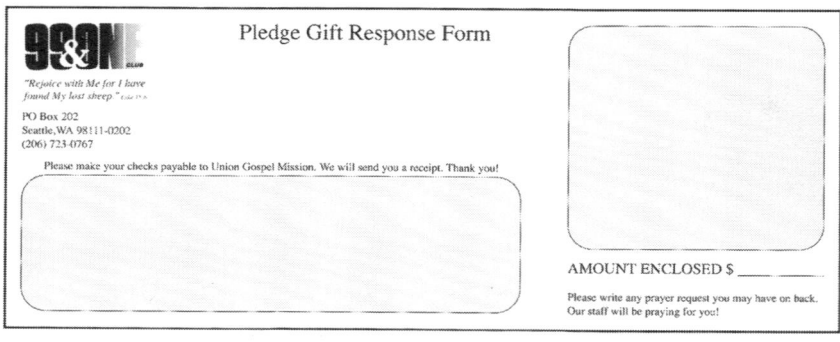

Pledge Gift Response Form

"Rejoice with Me for I have
found My lost sheep." (Luke 15:6)

PO Box 202
Seattle, WA 98111-0202
(206) 723-0767

Please make your checks payable to Union Gospel Mission. We will send you a receipt. Thank you!

AMOUNT ENCLOSED $ _____

Please write any prayer request you may have on back.
Our staff will be praying for you!

Pledge gift response device (with dollar amounts)
Kokomo Rescue Mission, Kokomo, Indiana

Kokomo Rescue Mission
300 W. Mulberry
P.O. Box 476
Kokomo, IN
46903-0476

Please enclose your gift and this form in the envelope provided.

Yes, I accept your invitation to join the 99 and ONE Club, helping the hurting and hungry of our community.

Here is my first monthly pledge gift of:
☐ $15 ☐ $25 ☐ $50 ☐ $100 ☐ Other_____
(Be assured you may cancel your pledge at any time.)

Name _____

Address _____

City _____ State_____ Zip_____

Telephone number (   ) _____

Your number will not be used for telemarketing.

Pledge gift response device (no suggested dollar amount)
Portland Rescue Mission, Portland, Ore.

Friends of the Friendless Pledge Reminder*

Portland Rescue Mission
Mike Maksimowicz
PO Box 3713
Portland, OR 97208-3713
www.portlandrescuemission.org

* If you have already sent your monthly gift, we thank you!

Amount Enclosed: $ _____

❑ Please charge my gift to my credit card:
❑ Mastercard ❑ Visa ❑ Discover ❑ Amex

Card Number: _____ Exp. Date: _____

Signature: _____
To charge by phone call 503-MISSION,
or visit www.portlandrescuemission.org to give online

❑ Please send information on Electronic Funds Transfer.

❑ Please send me the Portland Rescue Mission monthly Prayer Letter.

❑ How can we pray for you? Share your request on reverse.

Name: _____
Street Address: _____
City, State Zip: _____

Prayer response device
Portland Rescue Mission, Portland, Ore.

Thank you for your faithful support of Portland Rescue Mission.
Your gift is tax-deductible to the full extent of the law. We will send a receipt for your records.

❑ I would like to receive information about the Mission via email whenever possible.

My email address is: _____
(example: yourname@serviceprovider.com, please print)

❑ I am interested in receiving general information on estate planning and the tax benefits of charitable gifts.

❑ Please pray for:

Monthly Partner Program brochures
Families Northwest, Bellevue, Wash., PAO, Issaquah, Wash.

A Monthly Program for Partners of **FAMILIES NORTHWEST**

family friends

families NORTHWEST
...because your family matters

Families Northwest,
formerly Washington Family Council,
is an independent, nor-for-profit
organization strengthening families
and the cultural support for marriage
through:

Research
Media
Resources
Strategies

VISION:
*For Washington State to become the
best place in the world to be married
and raise children.*

MISSION:
*To encourage and equip communities to
value marriage and strengthen families.*

PO Box 40584   Bellevue, WA 98015-4584
(425) 637-5959   Fax (425) 637-5955
www.familiesnorthwest.org

Electronic Giving Program **It's Simple**

Choose one of the two giving options below:

❏ Electronic Funds Transfer

I authorize my bank to transfer $ _____ from my account to *Families Northwest* monthly in accordance with the terms and conditions stated below. Please transfer my monthly gifts on the *(Check one)* ❏ 5th   ❏ 15th   ❏ 20th of every month.

Name of Bank _____   Account Number _____

Signature _____   Date _____

(Please include a voided check.)

❏ Credit Card

I authorize *Families Northwest* to charge $_____ to my credit card on or about the 10th of every month in accordance with the terms and conditions stated. Type of credit card   ❏ VISA   ❏ Mastercard

Name on Card_____   Credit Card Number _____   Expiration Date _____

Signature_____   Date _____

Thank You! Your first Electronic Funds Transfer or Credit Card Gift will occur within 45 days.

Yes! I want to become a *Family Friend.* I would like to pledge . . .

❏ *$20* ❏ *$30* ❏ *$50* ❏ *$75* ❏ *$100* ❏ *Other*_____

Name(s) _____

Address _____

City _____

State _____ Zip _____

Home Phone _____ Work Phone _____

Enclosed is my first pledge of $_____.

❏ I would like to sign up for the convenience of **Electronic Giving.** *(Please see reverse to sign up.)*

❏ I cannot become a *Family Friend* at this time, but please use my special one-time gift of $ _____ to help families, marriages, and children.

Families Northwest (formerly Washington Family Council) is a 501(c)3 organization; gifts are tax-deductible

---

Why become a Family Friend?

You will . . .

■ Know that you are playing a significant role in reversing the trends of family breakdown and helping to create a culture in Washington that values marriage and strengthens families

■ Take advantage of easy Electronic Giving or Monthly Reminders

■ Receive special invitations to *Families Northwest* events

■ Know that you are contributing to the financial stability of *Families Northwest*

■ Receive the *Family Friends* monthly update

■ Be able to spread our giving into installments

■ Receive membership materials

Your friendship with *Families Northwest,* expressed through your monthly gift, will make a significant difference for marriages and children in Washington State.

Convenient Electronic Giving

It's Direct

You can now make your monthly contribution to *Families Northwest* through direct Electronic Funds Transfer from your bank account or credit card. No need to write a check, find a stamp or mail your gift. You will still receive a tax-deductible receipt each month.

It's Convenient, Safe, Saves Time and Money

You won't have to worry about forgetting to make your monthly gifts. Electronic transfers are the most secure form of giving. Electronic Giving cuts down on record keeping and check processing costs. Therefore, your gifts are used more efficiently.

You Keep Control

You maintain control over your giving as always. At any time, just by sending a written notice, you can:

■ Change your donation amount

■ Cancel your donation

■ Change bank accounts

TERMS AND CONDITIONS

[fine print unreadable]

There is Hope

Everyday in Washington, thousands of kids go home from school to a fractured, hurting family. Divorce, domestic violence, and out-of-wedlock births are leaving many single parents in poverty. **But there is hope for the future of marriage and families in our state.** *Families Northwest* is working to address the epidemic of family breakdown at its root cause. We're building a marriage movement, implementing strategies and providing resources that will *make a difference* in the lives of couples, parents, and children for now, and in the future.

We Need You

Families Northwest needs friends to help us fight family breakdown before it starts by sharing our vision of making Washington State the best place in the world for families. That's why we've created *Family Friends;* a way for friends like you to support the mission of *Families Northwest* in an easy and effective way. By getting involved as a *Family Friend* and supporting us with a monthly gift, you will be helping to build a stronger, brighter, safer and more secure future for your neighbors and loved ones . . . *today.*

67

Monthly partners of

PRO ATHLETES OUTREACH

Join the Team

PAO's Vision:

To recruit and equip an army of professional athletes, coaches and their families to make a positive impact in the world for Jesus Christ

Monthly partners of

TEAMMATES

PRO ATHLETES OUTREACH

P.O. Box 1044
Issaquah WA 98027
425.392.6300
800-733-7306
office@pao.org
www.TheGoal.com

PRO ATHLETES OUTREACH

&

TEAMMATES

A winning combination!

Committed to reaching pro athletes, coaches and their families in this generation and the next.

Terms and Conditions

The authorization to charge your bank account or credit card is the same as if you had personally signed a check to Pro Athletes Outreach. This agreement will remain in effect until you write a letter to Pro Athletes Outreach requesting that we end this agreement. Please provide 30 days notice.

A record of your gifts will be included on your bank or credit card statement. Please review the statement carefully and notify Pro Athletes Outreach if you find an error in the transferred amount. We will correct it immediately. Also, if there is an error, you have the right to tell your bank to reverse any transfer. This must be done in writing to your bank within 15 days of the date on the bank statement, or within 45 days after the transfer has been made.

PRO ATHLETES OUTREACH

PO Box 1044
Issaquah, WA 98027
425-392-6302 425-392-7640 fax
office@pao.org   www.TheGoal.com

TEAMMATES

Who are Teammates?

Teammates are committed friends of PAO and its ministry to pro athletes, coaches, and their families. Teammates' monthly gifts will make a significant impact on the lives of these influential people for the cause of Christ.

Please join us as we

"Influence the Influencers"

together!

PAO is scouting for Teammates now!

What are the benefits of being a Teammate?

To Teammate Members:

- Knowing you are providing consistent support to the front lines of this ministry
- Regular prayer for you by PAO leadership staff
- A monthly update from Norm and Bobbe
- Convenient, automatic giving options of electronic funds transfer or credit card

To PAO:

- Consistent financial support from friends of PAO
- Encouragement knowing there are those who will stand in the gap with PAO

What will my faithful support do?

- Introduce pro athletes, coaches and their families to Jesus Christ
- Equip pro athletes, coaches and their families to model and cultivate Christ-like character qualities for those who are watching
- Strengthen marriages and relationships of pro athletes and coaches
- Equip pro athletes and coaches to honor God by living with integrity
- Provide networking, and ongoing encouragement and accountability for pro athletes, coaches and their families

"Influence the Influencers"

TEAMMATES

Monthly partners of PAO Pro Athletes Outreach

☐ **Yes, I would like to join Teammates!**

Name _____

Address _____

City _____ State ____ Zip ____

Phone (___) _____ Cell (___) _____

E-mail: _____

I would like to pledge $ _____ per month.
(Please choose one of the three options listed below.)

☐ I will send a check each month.
You will receive a pledge reminder with an envelope at the beginning of each month.

☐ Electronic Funds Transfer (EFT)
I authorize my bank to transfer $ _____ from my account to PAO monthly in accordance with the Terms and Conditions stated on the back of this form.

Please transfer my monthly gift on the (check one) ☐ 5th or ☐ 20th of every month.

I am enclosing a voided check to begin the process. I understand that my first EFT will occur within 45 days.

Signature _____

Date _____

☐ Credit Card / ☐ Debit (Card must have Visa/MC logo.)
According to the Terms and Conditions on the back of this form I authorize PAO to charge $ _____ each month to my credit card. ☐ Visa ☐ MasterCard
(The charge will take place the 20th of each month.)

Credit Card Number _____ Exp. Date ____

Signature _____

Additional Resources

As you create your Monthly Partner Program, you can receive additional insights and helps from these respected organizations:

EDMI Publishing	800-255-EDMI
Christian Stewardship Association	www.stewardship.org
EFTPlus	www.eftplus.com
EFT Corporation	www.etransfer.com
Association of Fundraising Professionals	www.afpnet.org

About the Authors

John Frank is President of John R. Frank Consulting Group, a comprehensive consulting firm helping nonprofit organizations set a course for success in development, management and leadership. A Certified Fund Raising Executive, John has led development efforts in rescue missions, Christian higher education, primary and secondary education, and international evangelism organizations. John is a nationally-recognized speaker and teacher, and his expertise includes current giving, capital campaigns, and leadership. He also consults with boards and ministry leadership.

John is a member of the faculty for international, national, and regional training conferences, graduate school courses, and the AGRM Rescue College Online Fundraising Course, the first of its kind in the country.

He has authored articles on development and leadership. His first book, *The Ministry of Development*, was published in 1996. He is also a contributing author to *From Soup & a Sermon to Mega-Mission, A Guide to Financing Rescue Missions.*

John was honored with the 2003 Excellence in Integrity Award from Campbell Research in their study of consultants to nonprofit organizations. He was profiled on CNN Headline News for receiving the Pat Summerall Champions of Industry Award in September 2003.

John holds a master's degree in Philanthropy and Development from Saint Mary's University, Winona, Minnesota. He and his family live in Woodinville, Washington.

To contact John, visit www.JohnRFrank.com.

Mark Cutshall specializes in helping leaders and organizations tell their story. He has co-authored eight books. He can be reached at mcutsh@aol.com.

71